Laughin' Jammin' Slammin' Jokefest

Backpack-Sized Laughs

Jacqueline Horsfall & Terry Pierce

STERLING

New York / London
www.sterlingpublishing.com/kids

Library of Congress Cataloging-in-Publication Data Available

8 10 9

Published by Sterling Publishing Co., Inc.
387 Park Avenue South, New York, NY 10016

Illustrated by Buck Jones, Mark Zahnd, Rob Collinet, Sanford Hoffman,
Lance Lekander. and Jackie Snider.

Material in this collection was adapted from *Joke & Riddle Ballyhoo* (text © by
Jacqueline Horsfall, illustrations copyright © by Jackie Snider), *Kids' Silliest
Jokes* (text © by Jacqueline Horsfall, illustrations by Buck Jones), *Super Goofy
Jokes* (text © by Jacqueline Horsfall, illustrations copyright © by Rob Collinet),
Greatest Goofiest Jokes (text © by Terry Pierce, illustrations by Buck Jones),
Funniest Riddle Book in the World (illustrations by Sanford Hoffman), *Kids'
Silliest Riddles* (illustrations by Buck Jones), *Ridiculous Riddles* (illustrations
by Mark Zahnd), *Kids' Kookiest Riddles* (illustrations by Rob Collinet),
Dr. Knucklehead's Knock-Knocks (illustrations by Lance Lekander),
Kids' Silliest Knock-Knocks (illustrations by Buck Jones), and *Ridiculous
Knock-Knocks* (illustrations by Mark Zahnd).

© 2007 by Sterling Publishing Co., Inc.
Distributed in Canada by Sterling Publishing
c/o Canadian Manda Group, 165 Dufferin Street,
Toronto, Ontario, Canada M6K 3H6
Distributed in the United Kingdom by
GMC Distribution Services,
Castle Place, 166 High Street, Lewes,
East Sussex, England BN7 1XU
Distributed in Australia by Capricorn Link (Australia) Pty. Ltd.
P.O. Box 704, Windsor, NSW 2756, Australia

Printed in China   01/13
All rights reserved

Sterling ISBN-13: 978-1-4027-4991-9
ISBN-10: 1-4027-4991-0

For information about custom editions, special sales, premium and
corporate purchases, please contact Sterling Special Sales
Department at 800-805-5489 or specialsales@sterlingpub.com.

Contents

1. Rise and Whine....5

2. Nature Noodles....14

3. Animal Crackers....35

4. People Pranksters....60

5. Computer Chuckles....77

6. Silly School....78

7. Funny Food....98

8. Open Wide!....122

9. Rap It Up, Please....136

10. Games & Groans....146

11. Mall Madness....158

12. Crazy Celebrations....172

13. Creepy Critters....190

14. Boo! Bloopers....203

15. Freaky Fairy Tales....227

16. Bathtime Belly Laughs....237

17. Bedtime Ballyhoo....264

18. Moon Madness....289

19. Night Mares....296

20. Grab Bag Gags....314

21. I'm Out of Here!....330

Index....344

1.
Rise and Whine

Why was the crab crabby
when he woke up?

The sea snore kept him up all night.

Why was the broom late?

It overswept.

*

Why did the worm oversleep?

*So it wouldn't get caught by
the early bird.*

*

Why did Silly Sarah take yeast
and furniture polish to bed?

So she'd rise and shine.

*

How do bees get to school
in the morning?

On the school buzz.

What did the bread do
when it woke up?

Loafed around.

*

What did Obi-Wan Kenobi say to
Luke Skywalker at breakfast?

Use the fork, Luke.

*

How do trees feel after a
good night's sleep?

Re-leafed.

*

What do nuts say when
they're angry?

*"Why don't you pecan someone
your own size?"*

BREAK YOUR FAST

What do cheerleaders eat
for breakfast?

Cheer-ee-ohs!

*

What do race car drivers eat
for breakfast?

Fast food.

*

What do cats eat for breakfast?

Mice Krispies.

*

What do canaries eat for breakfast?

Cream of tweet.

What happened when the dog
swallowed an alarm clock?

It got a lot of ticks.

*

How do you know when your
alarm clock is hungry?

It goes back for seconds.

TIME TO GET UP

What time does a shark get up?
Ate o'clock.

What time does a doctor get up?
Sicks o'clock.

What time does a dentist get up?
Tooth hurty.

What time does a tennis
player get up?
Ten-ish.

What time does a duck get up?
At the quack of dawn.

2.
Nature Noodles

What's the richest kind of air?
Billionaire.

*

What would you get if
worms ruled the earth?
Global worming.

*

Why do lightning bugs
get A's in school?
They're very bright.

Where do worms get their mail?
At the compost office.

What trees make good pets?
Dogwoods and pussy willows.

Why do pine trees
love winter?

They can wear their fir coats.

*

What kind of tree likes
doing housework?

A sweeping willow.

*

What kind of flower
is in your eye?

An iris.

Which insects have the
best manners?

Ladybugs.

*

Why shouldn't you tell secrets
in a room full of beetles?

Because the room is bugged.

*

What's a flea's favorite plant?

A cattail.

*

What's a flea's second
favorite plant?

Dogwood.

How do lobsters get to the airport?
By taxi crab.

What insect can tell time?
A clockroach.

*

Why don't ants smell?
They wear deodor-ant.

*

What goes buzz, buzz, buzz, plop?
A bee laughing its head off.

*

What do honeybees use to
check out flowers?
Bee-noculars.

WACKY NATURE BOOKS

How to Catch Butterflies
by Annette N. Ajar

Collecting Clams and Mussels
by Shelley Beech

My Life as a Lumberjack
by Tim Burr

Safe Winter Driving
by I. C. Rhodes

Why Bees Love Flowers
by Polly Nation

What do butterflies become after they graduate from college?

Mothematicians.

*

What do ants furnish their homes with?

Ant-iques.

*

What do riverbanks do their homework in?

Their notebrooks.

If a buttercup is yellow,
what color is a hiccup?

Burple.

*

Why don't mountains
get cold in winter?

Because they wear snowcaps.

*

Which flowers are happy
to see you?

Glad-iolas.

How do police get rid
of mosquitoes?

They call out the SWAT team.

Why did the silly boy take his piggy bank outdoors?

He heard there was going to be a change in the weather.

*

What should you do if you fall off your bicycle?

Get back on and re-cycle.

*

What falls on a mountain but never gets hurt?

Snow.

If two snakes marry, what will
their towels say?

Hiss and Hers.

What did the mountain scream
after the earthquake?

"It wasn't my fault!"

*

What did Papa Pig put on his face
when he cut himself shaving?

Oink-ment.

*

How did the chimp fix the
leaky faucet?

With a monkey wrench.

Why did Silly Billy stand
before the bathroom mirror
with his eyes shut?

*He wanted to see what he
looked like asleep.*

*

What would you do if you broke a
tooth while flossing?

Use tooth paste.

*

Why did Silly Billy sign up his
aquarium for army duty?

*He heard they needed
more tanks.*

Why did Silly Sarah take
a rabbit to the bathroom?

She wanted to blow-dry her hare.

Why did Silly Sarah take trees
to the bathroom?

To wash off her dirty palms.

*

Why did the moose pose
in the bathroom mirror?

To flex his big mooscles.

*

Why did the male deer smile
in the bathroom mirror?

To show off his buck teeth.

How do you divide the
sea in half?

With a sea saw.

*

How do beetles clean
their teeth?

*They chew sugar-free
buggle gum.*

*

Which wild animal is
a hair stylist?

Bullwinkle the Mousse.

What did the little lobster
get on its math test?

Sea-plus.

*

How do oysters get ready
for work?

*They wake up pearly
in the morning.*

*

How do eels get out of
a muddy seabed?

With 4-eel drive.

Where do jellyfish sleep?
In tent-acles.

*

Where do sea horses sleep?
Near barn-acles.

*

Why does Neptune
wear a tank top?
To show off his mussels.

*

What do you call a dandelion
floating in the ocean?
Sea weed.

3.
Animal Crackers

What kind of plane does
an elephant fly?

A jumbo jet.

What do you call sheep that
join law enforcement?

The Fleece Police.

*

What's a kangaroo's favorite year?

Leap year.

*

What kind of cars do
hummingbirds drive?

Hum-vees.

*

Why didn't the alligator finish
its homework?

It was swamped.

What do you call a crocodile that lives between two buildings?

An alley-gator

What's a crocodile's favorite drink?

Gatorade.

*

Where do rabbits get their food?

At hopping centers.

*

What do you call a lizard
that wins the lottery?

A chamelionaire.

*

What do seals wear with
their bathrobes?

Bedroom flippers.

What animal is smarter than
a talking parrot?

A spelling bee.

*

What do you call a tiger
in the snow?

A cool cat.

*

What's a giraffe's favorite fruit?

Neck-tarines.

*

What do skunks become after
they take a bath?

Ex-stinked.

What's the first thing a dolphin
learns at school?

Her A-B-Seas.

Why do dolphins swim
in salt water?

Pepper makes them sneeze.

*

How do chickens get
into college?

By passing their eggs-aminations.

What happened when the cat
ate a ball of yarn?

She had mittens.

*

What's a cat's favorite TV show?

The Evening Mews.

*

When is it bad luck to have a
black cat following you?

When you're a mouse.

*

How do mice revive each other?

*With mouse-to-mouse
resuscitation.*

What do mice use
for bad breath?

Mousewash.

*

What would you get if a 50-ton
duck stomped on the ground?

An earthquack.

*

What kind of dogs do
vampires own?

Bloodhounds.

WACKY ANIMAL BOOKS

Why Cats Scratch
by Manny Fleeze

Keep Your Pet Healthy
by Ray B. Shott

How To Build a Better Mousetrap
by Kit E. Katt

Why We Love Garbage Cans
by Al E. and Tom Katt

Dogs Running Wild
by Ty M. Upp

What's a cow's favorite movie?
"The Sound of Moooosic."

*

What's a crayfish's favorite movie?
"Fiddler Crab on the Roof."

*

What do you call a pig
flying a helicopter?
A pork chopper.

*

What kind of spaceship
do sheep fly?
Ewe F. Os.

Why do moths make good actors?

*They're attracted to
the spotlight.*

*

Where do butterflies go to dance?

The mothball.

*

What's a ladybug's favorite
singing group?

The Beetles.

*

Where do spiders get
their music?

On the Web.

Why did the whale cross
the ocean?

To get to the other tide.

49

What do you call
a lazy kangaroo?

A pouch potato.

What should you give a snake
before putting it to bed?

A good-night hiss.

*

What does a cheetah get
when it hits its head?

A CAT scan.

*

What do you get when your pet
goldfish jumps out of its bowl?

Sushi.

*

What time do chickens wake
up in the morning?

Five o'cluck.

What did the rooster crow
after a pasta dinner?

"Cock-a-noodle-doo!"

*

What do sea creatures
eat on their birthdays?

Crab cakes.

*

What do cats eat on
their birthdays?

Mice-cream cones.

*

What do you call a cat
that drinks bad milk?

Sourpuss.

What animal should you never
play cards with?

A cheetah.

How do you videotape
a beach party?

With a clamcorder.

*

What do crabs say when they're
introduced at beach parties?

"Shell we dance?"

*

How do sharks introduce
themselves at beach parties?

"Pleased to eat you."

*

How is the letter A
like a rosebush?

*They both have bees
coming after them.*

Where do you find frogs
at football games?

On the cheerleaping squads.

How does Zorro protect
himself from sharks?

With a swordfish.

Why can't you tell pigs
your secrets?

They squeal.

*

How do hogs haul their garbage?

In pig-up trucks.

*

What do you call a pig in the
middle of the highway?

A road hog.

*

Why aren't frogs allowed
at baseball games?

They eat all the fly balls.

How do dinosaurs like their prey?
Terrifried!

*

What's the best way to keep a
skunk from smelling?
Plug its nose.

*

What marks a turkey's burial site?
A gravystone.

*

Why do flamingos stand
on one leg?
*If they stood on no legs,
they'd fall down!*

What helps Santa fly safely through hurricanes?

His rain deer.

*

When are chickens penalized at basketball games?

When they cross the fowl line.

4.
People
Pranksters

Why are pizza makers so wealthy?

They're always rolling in dough.

Why would Snow White
make a good judge?

She's the fairest of them all.

*

What kind of car does
Mickey Mouse drive?

A Minnie van.

*

How did the lumberjack
chop down a tree?

Axedentally.

C'MON IN!

How do you welcome
a skydiver?

"Glad you could drop in!"

How do you welcome a sailor?

"Nice to sea you."

How do you welcome
a centipede?

*"Put your feet, feet, feet, feet,
feet, feet up."*

How do you welcome an angel?

"Halo there, c'mon down!"

What did the lamp say when the owner turned it off?

"Thanks a watt!"

*

Why did everyone laugh at the biologist?

He bent over and split his genes.

*

What do scientists do after they discover a new gene?

Cell-ebrate!

Why did the farmer plow
his field with a steamroller?

He wanted to grow mashed potatoes.

WACKY LIBRARY BOOKS

I Can Do Anything
by Will Power

How to Get Along with Your Sister
by Sharon Sharealike

The Unfinished Story
by Cliff Hanger

Why Amy Walked to School
by Mr. Bus

Oops, I Did It Again!
by Miss Take

Embarrassed in the Shower
by Kurt N. Fell

How did the farmer mend
his jeans?

With a cabbage patch.

*

What do you call a chicken farmer?

An eggspert.

*

Where do hogs live at
the North Pole?

In pigloos.

*

What do you call a princess
with a tidy house?

Sweeping Beauty.

What did the driver say when
she couldn't stop?

"Give me a brake!"

*

Who invented a plane that
couldn't fly?

The Wrong Brothers.

Why don't scuba divers
make good grades?

They're always below C-level.

SILLY SMOOCHIES

What did the mitten
say to the hand?

"I glove you very much."

What did the bee say to the rose?

"You're my honey."

What did the salt say to the sugar?

"How did you get so sweet?"

What did the lipstick
say to the mascara?

"Let's kiss and makeup."

What did the bubble gum
say to the shoe?

"I'm stuck on you."

What was the diver doing
in his garage?

Changing his shark plugs.

*

Why did the biologist stop
feeding dolphins?

She didn't see the porpoise in it.

*

How did the police officer know
the suspects stole the ketchup?

He caught them red-handed.

*

How do carpenters
greet each other?

"House it going?"

What do you get when a police officer surprises a skunk?

Law and odor.

What do you call a genius pig?

Einswine.

What did the contractor say when
his electrician came to work
at noon?

"Wire you insulate?"

*

Why was Einstein's head wet?

He had a brainstorm.

*

What kind of scientist
invented soda pop?

A fizzicist.

YOU'RE KRAZY, KID!

What did the squirrel say to
the acorns?

"Are you nuts?"

*

What did the math teacher say
to her student?

"What's your problem?"

*

What did the mechanic say
to the truck engine?

"You've got a screw loose, buddy!"

What's a snowboarder's least
favorite season?

Fall.

*

What's a lifeguard's
favorite game?

Pool.

*

Why are astronauts banned
from pools?

They make too many splashdowns.

*

What's another name for
submarine pilots?

Deep sea drivers.

Why are so many baseball
players in jail?

They're always stealing bases.

Who do you call when beach boys
won't go to sleep?

The Sandman.

Why do carpenters have bad teeth?
They're always biting their nails.

*

What do umpires say when their
cakes explode in the oven?
"Batter up!"

*

What's the first thing a karate
instructor does on an airplane?
Fastens his black belt.

*

How does a minister pray when
he has a cold?
On his sneeze.

5.
Computer Chuckles

How do train conductors find information on the Internet?

They use a search engine.

What did one keyboard say to
the other keyboard?

"You're not my type."

*

What kind of chips are found in
farmers' computers?

Potato chips.

*

What do computers do in
the cafeteria?

Take a byte.

*

What equipment do aardvarks
buy with their software?

Aardware.

What should you do if your
computer crashes?

Take away its driver's license.

*

What's an astronaut's favorite
computer key?

The space bar.

WEIRDO WEBSITES

Have you seen the
leopard website?

No, I haven't spotted it yet.

*

Have you seen the
hurricane website?

It really blew my mind!

*

Have you seen the
goldfish website?

It really bowled me over!

Have you seen the
fishing website?

It isn't online yet.

*

Have you seen the
boxing website?

It knocked me out!

*

Have you seen the
tomato website?

I'll ketchup with it later.

*

Have you seen the
opticians' website?

It's a site for sore eyes.

Have you seen the
mountain website?

I must take a peak.

*

Have you seen the
paper towel website?

It's very absorbing.

*

Have you seen the
boomerang website?

You'll go back to it again and again.

*

Have you seen the lions
and tigers website?

I'm not wild about it.

Why do beavers spend so much
time on the Internet?

They never want to log off.

*

Where do snowmen put
their websites?

On the Winternet.

Why did the computer sneeze?
It had a virus.

*

What do you call a grandmother
who designs programs?
A computer programma.

*

What's a carpenter's favorite
computer icon?
The toolbar.

*

What do computer programmers
do on weekends?
Go for disk drives.

WACKY COMPUTER BOOKS

How to Clean Your Computer
by Dusty Keebord

How to Fix Spelling Mistakes
by Dee Leete

Set Up Your Own Website
by Dot Comm

How to Get a High-Tech Job
by Bea A. Nerd

*The World's Largest
Software Company*
by Mike Rosoft

What would you get if you crossed
a computer with a ballerina?

The Netcracker Suite.

*

How can you learn ballet dancing
on the Internet?

Use the tutu-torial.

*

What do you get if a tarantula
sits on your computer?

A spider byte.

*

How does Old MacDonald
send messages?

By e-i-e-i-o-mail.

How do Italian cooks swap recipes?

By spaghett-e-mail.

*

Why was the chicken banned
from sending e-mails?

*She was always using
fowl language.*

*

How do e-books communicate?

They page each other.

6.

Silly School

In what school do you greet people?

"Hi!" school.

How can you tell if
math teachers dye their hair?

You can see their square roots.

*

What do music teachers
tell their students?

To B-sharp.

*

What do students learn
in night school?

To read in the dark.

*

When do students fail driver's ed?

When they're in a no-passing zone.

What should you tell your
favorite gym teacher?

"This class is a ball!"

*

Why was the moth afraid to give
an oral book report?

It had butterflies in its stomach.

*

What do you call a kitten that
borrows your homework?

A copy cat.

What should you tell your
favorite geology teacher?

"This class rocks!"

*

What should you tell your
favorite math teacher?

"You're number one!"

Where did Sir Lancelot learn
to slay dragons?

In knight school.

*

Why are English teachers helpful?

*They always give the
write answers.*

*

Why do students attend
summer school?

Summer smart, summer dumb.

*

What's the best way to get
rid of a bad grade?

Erase it.

What do hog students write with?
Pigpens.

*

Where do hogs keep their
lunch money?
In piggy banks.

YOUR ATTENTION, PLEASE!

What did the teacher say
to the eyeball?

"Are you one of my pupils?"

What did the teacher say to
the hot dog buns?

"Time for roll call!"

What did the teacher say
to the golfer?

"Can you count to fore?"

What did the teacher say to the elf?

"Did you finish your gnomework?"

What did the teacher say to the octopus?

"Please raise your hand, hand, hand, hand, hand, hand, hand, hand."

What kind of stories do little
horses read in kindergarten?

Ponytales.

*

Where do religious-school
students have recess?

On the prayground.

*

Why do principals always
visit math classes?

They're the rulers of the school.

*

Where do chickens find
information for their term papers?

In the hencyclopedia.

What's the best paper to write
in a stream?

Your brook report.

*

How do fish paint in art class?

With watercolors.

*

What's the most important thing to
write on a test?

Your name.

7.
Funny Food

What does an astronaut eat
her spaghetti from?

A satellite dish.

What do you get when you spill
soda in a cornfield?

Popcorn.

*

What do penguins put
in their salad?

Iceberg lettuce.

*

What do ship captains put
on their salad?

Crew-tons.

*

What would you get if you dropped
a French fry on the sofa?

A couch potato.

How do you know when there's a
turkey in your refrigerator?

All the food is gobbled up.

What are penguins'
favorite fast food?

Icebergers.

*

What do you call a funny book
about eggs?

A yolk book.

*

What's a spider's favorite
picnic food?

Corn-on-the-cobweb.

*

How can you tell if a
clock is hungry?

It goes back four seconds.

LET'S EAT OUT!

What did the cream say
to the mixer?

"I'm beat!"

What did the spaghetti say to
the cheese at midnight?

"It's pasta my bedtime."

What did the hot dog say
to the barbecue?

*"I'd like you to meat
my grillfriend."*

What did the turkey say
to the stuffing?

"I'm stuffed!"

What did the broth say to
the vegetables?

"You're souper!"

What did the beef say
to the oven?

*"Turn down the heat...
I'm roasting!"*

What kind of cake is served
in a haunted house?

Eye scream cake.

What kind of fruit do
shellfish eat?

Crab apples.

*

What do quarterbacks like
to do at dinner?

Pass the salt.

*

What kind of salt do gymnasts use?

Somersault.

*

What do you call
fifteen-year-old salt?

A salt-teen.

What do you get when
a waiter trips?

Flying saucers.

*

Where do vegetables volunteer?

The Peas Corp.

*

Why are potatoes good detectives?

*They always keep their
eyes peeled.*

*

What does a porcupine put on
its submarine sandwich?

Dill prickles.

What do alligators cook in?

Croc-pots.

Where do bad vegetables go?

To the re-farm-atory.

*

Why do frogs have such
an easy life?

*Because they eat whatever
bugs them.*

*

What should you do with
rude pepperoni?

Give it a pizza your mind.

SHUT THE DOOR... I'M DRESSING!

What dressing does Popeye
put on his salad?

Olive Oyl.

What dressing do nice cows
put on their salad?

Honey Moostard.

What dressing do cowboys
put on their salad?

Ranch.

What dressing do sad people
put on their salad?

Blue Cheese.

What dressing do cruise
directors put on their salad?

Thousand Island.

What dressing does a Cyclops
put on its salad?

Screamy Eyetalian.

Who wears a red cape and
leaps from restaurant roofs in
a single bound?

Supperman.

*

Who has friends for lunch?

A cannibal.

*

What did the teddy bear say
when offered dessert?

"No, thanks, I'm stuffed."

*

What's a chimp's favorite
ice cream?

Chunky Monkey.

Why did Silly Billy run
through the sprinkler with
his ice cream cone?

He wanted lots of sprinkles on top.

*

How do giant sequoias like
their ice cream served?

In pinecones.

*

What kind of fruit leaves
holes in your tongue?

A porcupineapple.

WACKY COOKBOOKS

The Best Pizza Ever
by Chris P. Krust

All About Peppers
by Holly Peenyo

Microwave Leftovers
by Luke Warmm

Outdoor Cooking
by Barbie Q.

Snacks for a Crowd
by Saul Ted P. Knotts

Yummy Christmas Treats
by Candy Kane

Healthy Vegetables
by Artie Choke

Where do baby eagles eat?
In high chairs.

*

Why did the silly student
eat his homework?
*The teacher said it would
be a piece of cake.*

*

What would you get if
potatoes took a bath?
Soapspuds.

*

What kind of vegetables could
help you fly a kite?
String beans.

What did one plate say to
the other plate?

"Lunch is on me!"

*

What kind of drink does Santa
bring bad boys and girls?

Coal-a.

*

What should farmers do if
crows steal their corn?

Call the crops.

Who leads the wedding party
when two bakers marry?

The flour girl.

What's the best snack to eat
in a swamp?

Marshmallows.

*

What do zookeepers eat
for snacks?

Animal crackers.

*

What do photographers
eat for snacks?

"Cheese!" sticks.

*

What do fathers eat for snacks?

Popcorn.

Why did the police raid
the refrigerator?

*The milk went bad and the
apples turned rotten.*

What award do you get for
eating your veggies?

The Nobel Peas Prize.

Where do crocodiles
store their food?

In refrigergators.

*

When should you put a
diamond ring in your soup?

When the recipe calls for carrots.

*

What should you do if
you have fat hair?

Dye it.

*

What do rock climbers
get their milk in?

Quartz.

8.
Open Wide!

How did the dentist
fix the dragon's teeth?

With a fire drill.

What has teeth but can't bite?

A comb.

*

What has 88 teeth but never brushes them?

A piano.

*

Why did the oak tree see a dentist?

To get a root canal.

*

What does a dentist tell in court?

"The tooth, the whole tooth, and nothing but the tooth."

What does a donkey wear to straighten its teeth?

Bray-ces.

*

What plant do you find in emergency rooms?

IV.

*

When do houses see a doctor?

When they have window panes.

*

Why did the basketball player go to the doctor?

He wanted to get more shots.

What do birds need when
they're sick?

Tweetment.

*

Why do doctors measure
snakes in inches?

Because snakes don't have feet.

CRITTER CHILLS

What should you send
a sick ghost?

A BOOquet of flowers.

Where should you send
a sick flea?

To a Lab.

Where can you find
a sick rabbit?

On a hopperating table.

How can you tell if a mummy
has a cold?

He starts coffin.

*

Where do dirty socks go
when they get sick?

To the Detergency Room.

MEDICAL BOOKS

How to Heal a Sore Throat
by Lauren Jitis

Shots Don't Hurt!
by Ben Dover

Malaria Symptoms
by Amos Quito

Veggies for Your Health
by Brock O'Lee

Clone Yourself!
by Gene Splitter

Everyday Dental Care
by Pearl E. Teeth

How to Cure Stomach Pain
by Tom E. Ake

Why can't a pony sing?
It's always a little horse.

What's the perfect cure
for dandruff?

Baldness.

What direction does
a sneeze travel?

Atchoo!

*

Where do cows buy their
cough drops?

At the farm-acy.

*

Why did the cow go to
the psychiatrist?

Because she was so moooody.

*

Why did the fireplace
call the doctor?

The chimney had the flue.

What sickness do
rodeo riders get?

Bronc-itis.

*

Why did the germ cross
the microscope?

To get to the other slide.

*

Why is an eye doctor
like a teacher?

They both test the pupils.

*

What is a drill sergeant?

An army dentist.

Why should you tiptoe past
the medicine cabinet?

So you won't wake the sleeping pills.

What's the healthiest
type of water?

Well water.

*

What means of transportation
gives people colds?

Achoo-choo train.

*

If an apple a day keeps the doctor
away, what will an onion do?

Keep everyone away.

*

Why did the cookie
go to the doctor?

It felt crumby.

What would you call a
small wound?

A shortcut.

*

If you don't feel well,
what do you probably have?

Gloves on your hands.

*

What did Captain Hook
do when he lost his hand?

He went to the second-hand shop.

9.
Rap It Up, Please

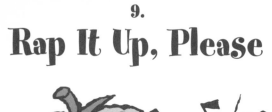

Where do strawberries
play their saxophones?

At jam sessions.

What kind of music
gets played at school?

Class-ical.

*

Who plays country music
at the beach?

The fiddler crabs.

*

Where does a daffodil hear its
favorite music?

On a bloom box.

What did the Pied Piper say
when he lost his flute?

"Oh, rats!"

*

What part does a grizzly sing
in the church choir?

Bearitone.

*

What musical instrument is found
in the bathroom?

A tuba toothpaste.

What do you call three oaks
who sing together?

A tree-o.

Which orchestra leader
has webbed feet?

The conducktor.

BAND AID

What instruments do
doctors play in a band?
Surgical ones.

What do surgeons
play in a band?
Organs.

What do turkeys
play in a band?

Drumsticks.

What do shoemakers play
in a band?

Soxophones.

What do skeletons
play in a band?

Trom-bones.

What do you call a dad who
sings and dances?

A Pop-star.

*

How is a movie like a broken leg?

They both need a cast.

*

Why couldn't the piano go home
after the concert?

It lost its keys.

*

What did the mother
piano say to the baby grand?

*"I don't like your tone,
young man."*

What do pianists use
to eat their steak?

Tuning forks.

*

Why was the pianist smacking
her head on the keys?

She was playing by ear.

*

Why do baseball players make
good pianists?

They have perfect pitch.

10.
Games & Groans

What's a baby's favorite ride?

A stroller coaster.

Why was Cinderella so
bad at basketball?

Her coach was a pumpkin.

*

How does Mother Earth fish?
With north and south poles.

*

Where do trains work out?
At the track.

*

How do locomotives work out?
With personal train-ers.

*

How do witches work out?
On hexercise machines.

Why did the pecan work out?
It was a health nut.

*

How do bees start
their exercises?
With swarm-ups.

HIT THE DECK

What card game do construction workers play?

Bridge.

What card game do anglers play?

Go Fish.

What card game do cardiologists play?

Hearts.

What card game do prisoners play?

Solitaire.

What's a tornado's
favorite game?

Twister.

*

What game do mice like to play?

Hide and squeak.

*

What's a baby sparrow's
favorite game?

Beak-a-boo.

*

What do you call wood that has
nothing to play with?

Board.

What do waiters ask
when playing tennis?

"May I serve?"

*

How do surfers greet each other?

With a tidal wave.

If Michael Jordan gets athlete's foot, what does Santa get?

Mistle toe.

*

Why did the police go to the baseball stadium?

They heard someone was stealing bases.

*

What position do camels play on baseball teams?

Humpire.

Why don't grasshoppers go to lacrosse games?

They prefer cricket matches.

*

Where should you sit at a ballpark if you want your clothes to get really white?

In the bleachers.

SPLASHERS

How do veterinarians swim laps?
They do the dog paddle.

How do chiropractors swim laps?
They do the back stroke.

How do spiders swim laps?
They do the crawl.

How do caterpillars swim laps?
They do the butterfly.

Who won the race between two balls of string?

They were tied.

*

How do frogs protect their knees when skateboarding?

They wear lily pads.

*

How do rubber bands warm up?

They stretch.

*

What exercise does your nose do when you have a cold?

It runs.

What game do falcons play on ice?
Hawk-ey.

*

How do pandas ride bikes safely?
They hold onto the handlebears.

What did one dumbbell say
to the other?

"Hey, weight for me!"

11.
Mall Madness

When skunks go for groceries, where do they find the best bargains?

At shopping scenters.

Why don't bumblebees
go shopping?

They're too buzz-y.

*

What happened to the origami
shop that used to be on this block?

It folded.

*

Where do ghosts shop?

At boo-tiques.

*

Where do streams buy
their novels?

At the brookstore.

How do grizzlies try on shoes?

Bearfoot.

*

What shoes should you buy when your basement is flooded?

Pumps.

*

What did the shoe say to the foot?

"You're putting me on!"

*

Where do sailors return damaged masts?

To the sails clerk.

What kind of pens do skunks buy?

Ones with indelible stink.

*

What kind of sneakers do
birds buy?

Ones with vel-crow.

How do kangaroos add up
their purchases?

With pocket calculators.

*

What do you call a kangaroo clerk
with bad manners?

Kangarude.

*

Where would you buy
thirty-six inches?

At a yard sale.

*

What does a house buy
at the mall?

Address.

Where should you pay your
car repair bill?

At the crash register.

*

What do pigs buy for relaxing in
the backyard?

Ham-mocks.

*

What's an easy way to
double your money?

Look at it in a mirror.

WACKY SHOPPING BOOKS

Collecting Modern Paintings
by Art X. Ibit

Shopping on the Second Floor
by Ellie Vader

Department Store Courtesy
by May I. Helpyoo

The History of Footwear
by Buck L. Myshoo

Shoplifting: A Serious Problem
by Reed M. S. Wrights

Where do animals go when
they lose their tails?

To the retail store.

*

What did the duck say when
she bought lipstick?

"Please, just put it on my bill."

Why do department
stores like cats?

They're pre-furred customers.

Which customers avoid
early-bird sales?

Worms.

*

What happens to vacuum cleaners
at a busy mall?

They get pushed around.

*

Did you hear about the two
racing silkworms?

They ended up in a tie.

167

SHOP TILL YOU DROP!

What do frogs buy at the mall?
Open-toad sandals.

What do chimney sweeps
buy at the mall?
Sootcases.

What do clones buy at the mall?
Denim genes.

What do sheep buy at the mall?
Baaaath towels.

What do cats buy at the mall?
Purrfume.

What do bumblebees
buy at the mall?
Bee-kinis.

How do billboards talk?

In sign language.

*

How do leopards do
their shopping?

From cat-alogs.

*

Why did the bald man refuse
to buy a wig?

He didn't want toupee.

*

Why did the rabbit buy a house?

It was tired of the hole thing.

Why did the rabbit get a job at the grocery store?

It wanted a raise in celery.

12.
Crazy Celebrations

What did the rabbit buy his fiancée?

A 14-carrot ring.

Why did Benny Bee get married?

He finally found his honey.

*

What do farmers give their wives
when they marry?

Hogs and kisses.

*

What do maples give each other
when they marry?

Tree rings.

*

What did the pinky say
to the thumb?

"I think I'm in glove with you."

What do hamburgers give each
other when they marry?

Onion rings.

What happens when two angels get married?

They live harpily ever after.

*

Who gets married at a witch's wedding?

The bride and broom.

*

What do you call two married spiders?

Newly-webs.

What does a duck wear
to a wedding?

A duxedo.

*

Who do pelicans bring with them
to weddings?

Their gullfriends.

*

What does Hamlet eat
on his birthday?

Danish.

*

What do squirrels eat
on their birthdays?

Donuts.

CUT THE CAKE!

What do mice eat on
their birthdays?

Cheesecake.

What do rabbits eat on
their birthdays?

Carrot cake.

What do demons eat on
their birthdays?

Devil's food cake.

What do saints eat on
their birthdays?

Angel food cake.

What do dwarfs eat on
their birthdays?

Shortcake.

What do divers eat on
their birthdays?

Sponge cake.

What do grouchy cows eat
on their birthdays?

Sour cream cake.

What do carpenters eat on
their birthdays?

Pound cake.

What do police eat on
their birthdays?

Cop cakes.

What does an oyster do
on its birthday?

Shellabrate.

*

What do you always get on
your birthday?

One year older.

*

When do kangaroos celebrate
their birthdays?

In leap years.

*

What birthday game
do cows play?

Moooosical chairs.

What do you sing before a robin
blows out its candles?

"Happy Bird-day to You!"

*

Who should you call if you have a
hundred candles on your cake?

The fire department.

*

Why didn't the skeleton go
to the birthday party?

It had no body to go with.

183

PROM NIGHT

How did Molly Mare wear
her hair to the prom?

In a ponytail.

How did Brenda Baker wear
her hair to the prom?

In a bun.

How did Sarah Sow wear
her hair to the prom?

In pigtails.

How did Colleen Contortionist
wear her hair to the prom?

In a twist.

How did Benny Bee wear
his hair to the prom?

In a buzz cut.

What does Santa eat first out of his Easter basket?

Belly beans.

*

What do tarantulas drink on Halloween?

Apple spider.

*

What do turkeys dress up as for Halloween?

Gobblins.

*

What do canaries do on Halloween?

Trick or tweet!

WACKY CELEBRATION BOOKS

Some Day My Prince Will Come
by Crystal Slippers

How to Plan a Fun Party
by Will I. C. U. Thayer

My Favorite Easter Gift
by Pat A. Bunnee

Too Excited to Sleep!
by Eliza Wake

Belated Birthdays
by M. T. Handed

Holidays from A to Z
by Dick Shenary and Alfie Bett

What kind of parties do
bricklayers attend?

Cement mixers.

*

Did you hear about the party
in the basement?

It made the Best Cellar List.

*

What does a werewolf say when
the party's over?

"Fangs a lot for inviting me!"

189

13.
Creepy Critters

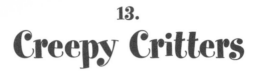

What should you wear when you
go to the beach with a monster?

Sunscream.

How do monsters call their moms
from the beach?

With shellular phones.

*

What beach creatures
do monsters turn into when
they get mad?

Crabs.

*

What's the best way to get
a unicorn's attention?

Honk its horn.

Where do ogres work
during the day?

At trollbooths.

What kind of bridge is too small
for a troll to live under?

The bridge of your nose.

*

Why can only one fairy sleep
under a toadstool?

*Because there isn't mushroom
under there.*

*

What do slugs put on their toes?

Snail polish.

194

Why was the troll so
good in art class?

He lived under a drawbridge.

*

What do ghosts read during
band practice?

Sheet music.

*

Where do baby ghosts sit
when they eat dinner?

In BOOster seats.

*

What's a witch's favorite
computer tool?

Spell check.

What does a witch do before she opens her e-mail?

Types in her passwart.

*

Why are spiders so popular online?

Each one has a Web site.

What talent does your cat have
if she can read your mind?

Extrasensory Purrception.

*

What kind of movies do frogs like?

Sci-fly.

*

Where should you take
Dracula on his birthday?

To a stakehouse.

*

Why is it fun to play baseball
with Dracula?

He has lots of bats.

EXCUSE MY BODY PARTS!

What did the skeleton
say to the doctor?

*"I hope this doesn't cost me
an arm and a leg!"*

What did the body say
to the skeleton?

"I've got you under my skin."

What did the heart say
to the liver?

"Let's beat it out of here!"

What did the throat say to
the bird-watcher?

"I think I just saw a swallow!"

What did the eye say
to the mouth?

*"One more word from you
and you'll get fifty lashes!"*

What do you call it when an extraterrestrial steals your jeans?

A clothes encounter.

What do scientists use to get
eels out of the ocean?

An eelbarrow.

*

What do slugs pack when
they go on a trip?

Sluggage.

*

Why do fleas never get cold?

They're always in fur coats.

*

When should you eat fireflies?

When you want a light snack.

What should you say to a
grumpy firefly?

"Lighten up!"

*

What do mice wear when
they shoot hoops?

Basketball squeakers.

*

Why do snakes ask
for spoons?

*Their tongues are
already forked.*

*

What do scorpions put
on their hot dogs?

Scorpionions.

14.

Boo! Bloopers

How do you know when there's
a dinosaur under your bed?

Your nose touches the ceiling.

What's the best way to get a
demon out of your bedroom?

Exorcise a lot.

*

Why do monsters use mouthwash?

They like to gargoyle.

*

What do ghosts put on first
thing in the morning?

Their boojeans.

*

What did the ghost say when it
floated through the bedroom wall?

*"Pardon me. I'm just
passing through."*

Who gave King Tut his bath?
His mummy.

*

Why do vampires gargle?
So they won't have bat breath.

BREAKFAST IN BED

What do ghosts order?

*Ghosted oats, raisin ghost, and a
boo-berry muffin.*

What do witches order?

*Sand-witch spread with
black cats-up, deviled eggs,
and low-fat I scream.*

What do ghouls order?

*Stir-fright vegetables, screamed
corn, and scare-ot cake.*

What do vampires order?

Mushroom bites, artichoke hearts with screamy yogurt dressing, T-bone stakes, and neck-tarines.

What does Bigfoot order?

Smashed potatoes and squash.

What does Bigfoot climb to
get to his bedroom?

Mon-stairs.

*

Why do witches hide under
your bed?

They love to play hide-and-shriek.

*

What do witches ask for when
they stop at a hotel?

A broom with a view.

*

What does a T. Rex do
when it sleeps?

Dino-snores.

What's hairy, fanged,
and 4-feet tall?

An 8-foot werewolf taking a bow.

Why did Dracula walk
around in his pajamas?

Because he didn't own a bat robe.

*

Why was the little ghost trapped
in the linen closet?

Its mom folded its sheet.

*

What do you say to quiet a
ghost under your bed?

*"Please don't spook until you're
spooken to."*

*

What wears an eyepatch and
robs ships at night?

A vampirate.

What did Mama Ghost say to her children when they got in the car?

"Fasten your sheetbelts."

*

What bedtime story does Mama Ghost read to her children?

"Ghouldilocks and the Three Bears."

*

What would you get if Bambi met a ghost under your bed?

Bamboo.

*

Why does Dracula want to meet your family?

He really likes the necks of kin.

Where do monsters sleep on
Halloween?

At the Howliday Inn.

*

What do you call a gorilla
wearing headphones?

Anything. He can't hear you.

Why is the Blob always
the last one to bed?

Because when you ooze, you lose.

*

What do you say to a skeleton
before it eats breakfast?

"Bone appetit!"

*

What does Dracula read each
morning before breakfast?

His horror-scope.

*

Why was E.T. the Extraterrestrial
late for the sleepover?

He had to phone home.

What boy wizard magically
grew a beard each night?

Hairy Potter.

*

Why did the ghost hire a maid?

To change his sheets every day.

*

Why did the baby ghost cry
himself to sleep?

He had a boo-boo.

*

What do witches do after
a sleepover?

They go home for a spell.

What do witches use after
they've blow-dried their hair?

Scare-spray.

How does a witch know
what time to get up?

She looks at her witch watch.

*

What time would it be if ten ghouls
chased you in your sleep?

Ten after one.

*

What's a 500-pound vampire
hovering over your bed?

A huge pain in the neck.

*

Why couldn't the Swamp Thing
get out of the tub?

It got bogged down.

Why do witches think
they're funny?

*Every time they look into the
bathroom mirror, it cracks up.*

*

What should you say when you
meet a ghost in your bedroom?

"How do you boo?"

*

Do mummies like
being mummies?

Of corpse!

*

Where does a werewolf
like to hide?

In your claws-it.

Why did the werewolf take a bite
out of the tightrope walker?

*It wanted to have a
well-balanced diet.*

*

What did the little zombie
say to her father before she
went to bed?

"Goodnight, Dead-y."

*

What do ghosts wash
their hair with?

Shamboo.

Why do skeletons play piano?
Because they don't have organs.

*

How does a witch play loud music?
On her broom box.

What's a witch's favorite movie?

Star Warts.

*

What happens when a witch
breaks the sound barrier?

You hear a sonic broom.

How do you welcome a ghost
into your house?

"Come right in and have a sheet."

*

What kind of construction vehicle
does a ghost drive?

A screamroller.

*

How do ghosts avoid
computer eyestrain?

They wear their spooktacles.

*

What do baby ghosts turn on
before they go to bed?

Their frightlights.

What do baby ghosts get
when they fall down?

Boo-boos.

*

Who did Frankenstein
take to the prom?

His ghoulfriend.

*

Who brings Christmas
presents to werewolves?

Santa Claws.

*

Why did the werewolf read
The Lord of the Rings 50 times?

It was hobbit-forming.

What kind of boats do vampires like?
Blood vessels.

*

How do little vampires get to sleep?
They count Draculas.

*

Why was 6 afraid of 7?
Because 7-8-9!

*

What do you call a haunted wasp?
A zom-bee.

*

What do you call a cloned kitten?
A mew-tant life form.

WACKY HORROR BOOKS

Tarantulas on the Loose
by Isadore Open

How to Dig a Grave
by Barry D. Boddy

UFOs Are Real!
by A. Lee N. Bean

Trade-In Body Parts
by Frank N. Stein

Night of the Werewolf
by Harry Bakk

I Died of Fright
by Terry Fide

How do you catch a fairy?
By its fairy tail.

*

How are spiders like ducks?
They both have webbed feet.

*

How big are centipedes?
One hundred feet long.

*

What would you get if two
spiders wrestled?
Scrambled legs.

15

Freaky
Fairy Tales

Who is beautiful, gray, and wore
big slippers to the ball?

Cinderelephant.

What did Dorothy say while taking
a bubble bath in Oz?

"There's no place like foam."

*

How did Robinson Crusoe survive
after his boat sank?

*He used a bar of soap and washed
himself ashore.*

*

Who does Clark Kent turn into
when he takes a shower?

Soaperman.

*

Why did Cinderella's tub overflow?

*Her rubber duckie turned
into a pumpkin.*

What does Cinderella wear at the beach?

Glass flippers.

Who fell asleep in the bathtub
for a hundred years?

Rip Van Wrinkled.

*

What does Tinkerbell ride at
the amusement park?

The fairy-go-round.

*

What do you call a little bear
who never takes a bath?

Winnie-the-Phew!

*

How do you make bears listen
to bedtime stories?

*Take away the B, and
they're all ears.*

What was Camelot famous for?

Its knight life.

∗

Why was Sir Lancelot
always so tired?

*Because he worked the
knight shift.*

∗

Why did King Arthur's Round
Table have insomnia?

There were a lot of sleepless knights.

∗

Why did Sir Galahad take
a flashlight to bed?

*He was afraid to sleep without a
knight light.*

What happens to a worm that falls asleep in Sir Galahad's apple?

It wakes up in the middle of the knight.

*

What do you call Billy the Kid when he's home in bed with the flu?

A sick shooter.

*

Where do bedtime books sleep?

Under their covers.

*

Did you hear about the Old Woman Who Lived in a Slipper?

Her shoe was being soled.

What do bakers read to their
children at night?

Bread-time stories.

*

What newspaper do cows
read in bed?

The Evening Moos.

What would you get if you
crossed a dentist with a boat?

The Tooth Ferry.

*

What happened to the boy
who slept with his head
under his pillow?

The Tooth Fairy took all his teeth!

*

Why are Tooth Fairies so smart?

They gather a lot of wisdom teeth.

Who writes nursery rhymes while squeezing oranges?

Mother Juice.

*

Why did Old Mother Hubbard scream when she went to fetch her poor dog a bone?

When she got there, the cupboard was bear.

*

Who brings you a bowl of ice cream before she sends you to the ball?

Your Dairy Godmother.

Where does Santa Claus sleep
when he's traveling?

In a ho-ho-hotel.

*

Why was Miss Muffet's spider
such a nuisance?

It kept getting in the whey.

*

What does the
Headless Horseman ride?

A nightmare.

*

What bedtime story does Mama
Cow read to her babies?

"Goodnight Moooon."

16.
Bathtime Belly Laughs

What do you call an X that just got out of the bathtub?

A clean X.

What happened when Mickey
Mouse fell into the bathtub?

He came out squeaky clean.

*

What would you say to a skunk
that fell into your tub?

"Stink or swim!"

*

What happened to the skunk that
fell into the bathtub?

It stank all the way to the bottom.

*

 If a skunk sprayed
you, could you wash
it off in the tub?

Let's soap for the best.

Why won't a leopard take
a bath with you?

It doesn't want to come out spotless.

*

Why can't a herd of elephants
ever get really clean?

*Because they can't take
off their trunks.*

*

What fluffy bird calls
"whoo, whoo" while you dry off?

A hoot towel.

*

Why does Mom put corncobs
in the tub?

So you'll wash behind your ears.

Where do sailors take their baths?

In a tubmarine.

*

What happened when the rubber
duckie fell into the bathtub?

It quacked up.

What TV programs should you
watch in the bathtub?

Soap operas.

*

What do you take when you have
a cell phone in the bathroom?

Babble baths.

*

How does a bear test
its bath water?

With its bear (bare) feet.

*

Why was the giraffe in the
tub for ten hours?

Its mom told it to wash its neck.

Why did Silly Sarah race
to the bathroom?

*Her boyfriend told her he'd left
a ring in the tub.*

*

What disappears when you stand
up in the bathtub?

Your lap.

*

Why did Silly Billy wear
slippers in the bathtub?

He heard the bottom was slipper-y.

*

What did Bigfoot say when he sat
on his rubber duckie?

"I've got a crush on you."

What does a goose get when its
bath water is too cold?

People-bumps.

*

Where do fish wash up?

In the bass-tub.

What kind of toy does the
Godfather play with in the tub?

A thug-boat.

*

When can't you take a bath
on an airplane?

When the No Soaking sign is on.

*

Why did Silly Billy put ice cubes
in his father's tub?

Because he likes cold pop.

*

How many rubber duckies
can you put into an empty tub?

One. After that, the tub isn't empty.

What do bumblebees put
in the bathtub first?

Their bee-hinds.

*

What would you be if a shark
was in your bathtub?

Chicken of the sea.

What kind of sandwich sinks
to the bottom of the tub?

A sub.

*

Why did Mom test the bath water
before putting Silly Billy in?

To prevent son-burn.

*

What did Mama Mountain tell
her children in the bathtub?

*"Be sure to wash behind
your mountaineers."*

Where do good little engines
wash themselves?

Behind their engineers.

*

What happens to a cranberry when
you throw it into an icy bath?

It becomes a blue-berry.

*

How do you make an orange
giggle in the tub?

Tickle its navel.

What does a leopard say
in the shower?

"That really hits the spot."

Why did Ms. Centipede spend three months in the tub?

She was shaving her legs.

*

What lines did Shakespeare write while soaking in the tub?

"Tub be or not tub be, that is the question."

*

What happened to Silly Billy when he took a bath in the washing machine?

He got very agitated.

Why did Silly Billy take a shower?
Because the bathtub was too heavy.

Why did the police officer
pack a bar of soap?

The city had a high grime rate.

*

What's the best dessert
to eat in the shower?

Sponge cake.

*

What kind of cake makes you gag?

A cake of soap.

*

Where does a rabbit go for
a shampoo?

To a hare-dresser.

How can you keep your hair dry
in the shower?

Don't turn on the water.

*

If someone robbed you in the
shower, what would you be?

An eye wetness.

*

Where does a jogger like
to wash up?

Under running water.

*

What did the faucet say
to the shower?

"You're a big drip."

Which rock singer really,
REALLY needs a shower?

Mud-donna.

SINGING IN THE SHOWER

What Beatles song did the octopus sing in the shower?

"I Wanna Hold Your Hand, Hand, Hand, Hand, Hand, Hand, Hand, Hand."

*

What do fathers sing in the shower?

Pop.

*

What do goblins sing in the shower?

Rhythm and boos.

What does a mummy
sing in the shower?

Wrap.

What do angels sing
in the shower?

Soul.

*

What do computer programmers
sing in the shower?

Disc-o.

*

What do trapeze artists sing
in the shower?

Swing.

*

What do steel workers sing
in the shower?

Heavy metal.

What kind of opera star
sings in the shower?

A soap-rano.

*

What's a plumber's favorite song?

"Singing in the Drain."

*

Why did the shower bar turn red?

Its towel fell off.

*

Why did the minister wash
himself with a sponge?

He heard it was very hole-y.

What's the cleanest store in town?

The soapermarket.

*

Why did the rabbit wear
a shower cap?

It didn't want to get its hare wet.

What is the appropriate attire
for a wedding in the shower?

A wet suit.

*

What kind of dog washes its fur in
the shower?

A sham-poodle.

*

Why did the cowboy splash water
on the bathroom floor?

Just to horse around.

Did you hear about the soaking
wet pregnant woman?

Her friends gave her a shower.

*

What does a wasp apply
after a shower?

Bee-odorant.

*

What happened to Einstein
when he took a shower?

He was brain-washed.

What's a diploma?

*When the sink is stopped up,
you call diploma.*

*

What did the bathroom rug
say to the floor?

"I'm mat about you."

*

How does a robot shave?

With a laser blade.

*

Why was the plumber so tired?

He was drained.

Why couldn't the police catch
the bathroom burglar?

He stepped on the scales and got a weigh.

17.
Bedtime Ballyhoo

What does a slice of toast
wear to bed?

Jam-mies.

Where can you lie without being scolded?

In bed.

*

What do you take off last before getting into bed?

Your feet off the floor.

*

What would you wear to a graduation ceremony at night school?

A nightcap and nightgown.

*

Why did Silly Billy wear banana peels on his feet?

He needed a pair of slippers.

How long should a slipper be?

One foot.

*

What runs around all day and
lies under the bed with its
tongue hanging out?

A sneaker.

*

Why does Silly Sarah put rollers
in her hair before bed?

So she'll wake curly in the morning.

*

Why did the radish turn red?

It saw the salad dressing.

*

Why did Silly Billy wear
a helmet to bed?

So he could crash.

What would you do if you trapped
an elephant in your pajamas?

Make him take them off!

*

How did the court know the
judge was ready for bed?

He was wearing his robe.

Why is it good to have holes
in your underwear?

So you can put your legs through.

*

Why did King Arthur wear
a T-shirt to bed?

He couldn't find his knight-y.

*

How does the Best Man put his
kids to bed?

He tux them in.

*

What famous nurse wore her
pajamas all day long?

Florence Nightingown.

What do you have when your head
is hot, your foot is cold, and you
see spots before your eyes?

A polka-dot sock over your head.

*

Why did the golfer change
his socks?

He had a hole-in-one.

*

Why did the belt get arrested?

It held up a pair of pants.

*

What does a germ call his
very small robe?

A microbe.

How do birds exercise
before they go to bed?

They do worm-ups.

BED WEAR?

What do you wear at a sleepover?
A sleep overcoat.

Why did Silly Sarah wear
kangaroo pajamas?
So she could leap into bed.

What does Tony the Tiger
wear to bed?
Paw-jamas.

What do lawyers wear to bed?
Their briefs.

What do prize fighters
wear to bed?

Boxers.

What do Japanese people
wear to bed?

Tea-shirts.

Why did Silly Billy wear
Zorro's cape to bed?

So he could catch some Z's.

*

Why did Mozart compose
symphonies in bed?

He was writing sheet music.

*

What is a billow?

*What you sleep on when you
have a bad cold.*

*

What has a waterbed but
never rests?

A river.

What do you call a dog who sleeps
on top of your computer?

Browser.

What do you call a spy who sleeps
with a blanket over his head?

An undercover agent.

*

Why did pioneers sleep in
covered wagons?

*So they wouldn't have to wait
forty years for a train.*

*

Why did the yogi
sleep on a bed
of tacks?

*He didn't have time
to do his nails.*

Where would you get the
wood to make a bed?

From the slumberyard.

*

Why did the hockey
player stay in bed?

He had the chicken pucks.

*

Why did Silly Sally give
her sleepover guests
a hammer and saw?

*She wanted them to make
their own beds.*

BEDHEADS

What kind of bed does
Elvis sleep in?

King-size.

What kind of bed does
Cleopatra sleep in?

Queen-size.

What kind of bed does
a fish sleep in?

Bass-i-net.

What kind of bed do
oysters sleep in?

Waterbed.

What kind of bed do baby
apes sleep in?

Apri-cots.

What's the difference between
a baker and an elephant?

*One bakes the bread, the other
breaks the bed.*

*

What's the difference between
a river and a jogger?

*A river can run for miles and
never get out of its bed.*

*

Why did the beggar feel
like an old bed?

*Because everyone kept
turning him down.*

How do we know that most
flowers are lazy?

They're always in a bed.

What does a car get after driving
a very long distance?

Tire-d.

*

Why do you have to go to bed?

Because the bed won't come to you.

*

Why did Silly Sarah stay
in bed all day?

She wanted to conserve energy.

PRIME TIME

When do slugs watch TV?
During slime time.

What TV sets do zebras watch?
Black and white.

What TV programs
do cows watch
in bed?
Moo-vies.

Nonsense...

What movie do tigers watch?

"Claws Encounters of the Furred Kind."

*

Why is the sea restless?

It has rocks in its bed.

*

How does Mother Nature make her bed?

With sheets of rain and blankets of snow.

*

Why should you always take a baseball player along if you want to sleep outdoors?

To pitch the tent.

Did you hear the story about the crumpled bed?

It hasn't been made up yet.

When is your room like a military dining hall?

When it's a mess.

*

Why did the computer fall asleep?

It was tired from a hard drive.

*

What do tired computer programmers do?

They go home and crash.

*

What do VCR tapes do at night?

They unwind.

How quickly do eggs get
ready for bed?

They scramble.

*

Which mountain is
always sleeping?

Mount Everest.

What do you get when you
eat crackers in bed?

A crumby night's sleep.

*

Did you hear about the soldier
who bought a camouflage
sleeping bag?

He can't find it.

*

Why do cowboys sleep
on the range?

*There isn't enough room
on the refrigerator.*

18.
Moon Madness

What's big, bright, and silly?

A fool moon.

Which Olympic high-jumper can jump higher than the moon?

All of them. The moon can't jump.

*

Why did the astronaut wear a football helmet when he landed on the Moon?

He was making a touchdown.

*

What do you call grass on the moon?

AstroTurf.

How do you find a cow in space?
Follow the Milky Way.

MAN IN THE MOON

How does the Man in the
Moon cut his hair?

Eclipse it.

How does the Man in the
Moon wash up?

He takes a meteor shower.

How does the Man in the
Moon eat soup?

With a Big Dipper.

How do you know the Man in the Moon likes clear nights?

Because when the clouds disappear, the moon beams.

What does the Man in the Moon get when he plays "Jeopardy"?

The constellation prize.

Why did the Man in the Moon's pants fall down?

He forgot to wear his asteroid belt.

How do you know that Saturn has taken a bath in your tub?

It leaves a ring.

*

How does an astronaut
read in bed?

He flicks on a satellight.

*

How do you get a baby
astronaut to go to sleep?

You rock-et.

*

Why didn't the astronaut
eat breakfast?

*He wanted to wait until
launch time.*

If you were abducted in your sleep by aliens, how would they tie you up?

With astro-knots.

*

What do you call meteorites that don't hit the Earth?

Meteorwrongs.

*

What's the messiest constellation?

The Big Dripper.

19.
Night Mares

Why did the sheep get pulled over
by a state trooper?

They made a ewe turn.

Where do the sheep go after you count them?

To the baaaathroom.

*

How did Mary feel about her little lamb's insomnia?

She wasn't going to lose any sheep over it.

*

If a lamb slipped in the shower, how would you get it to the hospital?

By lambulance.

Why is it easier to count
cows than sheep?

You can use a cowculator.

*

What would you get if you crossed
a sheep and a monkey?

A baa-boon.

*

What do sheep do when they go
out on a date at night?

A little star-grazing.

*

What do lambs do if they can't fly?

Go by spacesheep.

What do you call the place where
they shear sheep?

A baa-baa shop.

*

Why couldn't the little lamb get up
in the morning?

It was still asheep.

*

Why is it hard to say your prayers
with a goat around?

It keeps butting in.

*

What toys do baby snakes
take to bed?

Their rattles.

What did the whale do when his
mom made him go to bed early?

He blubbered.

*

What time is it when an elephant
climbs into your bed?

Time to get a new bed.

What prayer do cows say
at bedtime?

"Do unto udders."

*

Why can't snakes say their
prayers before bed?

They don't have any knees.

*

What does Mama Snake give her
babies before they go to sleep?

Hugs and hisses.

*

What did the monkey say when his
tail got caught in the bedroom fan?

"It won't be long now."

Why did Mama Duck scold
her goslings?

For eating quackers in bed.

*

What animal pouts when it
has to go to bed?

A whinoceros.

*

Who stays with young squids when
their parents go out?

Baby-squidders.

*

Why shouldn't you put a four-leaf
clover under your pillow?

You don't want to press your luck.

What did the sleeping dog say
when he fell off the couch?

"W-oof!"

Why did Silly Sarah take a
bale of hay to bed with her?

To feed her night mare.

*

What happened when
Ms. Owl got a sore throat?

She didn't give a hoot.

*

How do you know Kermit the Frog
had a bad dream?

He toad you so.

306

What does Mama Pheasant say
when she kisses her children
goodnight?

"Pheasant dreams."

*

Where did Cinderella Spaghetti
dream she was going?

To the Meat Ball.

*

Why did Silly Sarah take
sugar to bed?

To have sweet dreams.

SWEET DREAMS

What movie do pigs
dream about?

"Jurassic Pork."

Which rock star do bumblebees
dream about?

Sting.

Which rock star does Sleeping
Beauty dream about?

Prince.

What movie star do travel agents dream about?

Tom Cruise.

Which rock group do exterminators dream about?

The Beatles.

What late-night host do post office workers dream about?

David Letter-man.

What do waiters dream about?

Sirloin tips.

What confusing dream did the Egyptian girl have?

She dreamed her daddy was a mummy.

*

How much does the Sandman charge you if you fall asleep on the beach?

A sand-dollar.

*

How does an ESP expert send his dreams?

With a sixth-sense stamp.

Why did the banana wear snore-
strips on his nose?

*He didn't want to wake up the rest
of the bunch.*

How do pigs communicate
their dreams?

In swine language.

*

Why did the baby goat cry when
he had a bad dream?

Because he was just a little kid.

*

Where do hockey players
dream of playing?

At the Empire Skate Building.

20.
Grab Bag Gags

Why do dogs giggle?
Because they're tick-lish!

Where should parents-to-be invest
their money?
In the stork market.

What's the difference between a chicken inspector and a skunk?

One smells fowl and the other is foul-smelling.

*

What did Mona Lisa say when she was hauled into court?

"I was framed!"

*

Why was the garbage man feeling so blue?

He was down in the dumps.

*

What would you get if you crossed a comedian and a frog?

A practical croaker.

RHYMING RIDDLES

What do you call a cat in love?

A smitten kitten.

What does a gorilla use to wrap packages?

Ape tape.

What do you call an insect that flies out of jail?

A free bee.

What do you call a dog that sneaks food off your plate?

A pooch mooch.

How do mystery writers hold up
their pants?

With suspensers.

*

What do farmers use to light
their fields at night?

A flarecrow.

*

Where do you clean a bat?

In the bat-tub.

Where did people dance in
Medieval times?

In knight clubs.

*

Which city is the joke capital
of America?

Omaha-ha, Nebraska.

Which composer do knights
like the most?

Moat-zart.

*

Why did the girl nibble on
her calendar?

She wanted a sundae.

*

Why are almond growers
paid so little?

Because they're good for nuttin'.

HOW DO YOU COMPLIMENT...?

How do you compliment the
Abominable Snowman?
Tell him he's cool.

How do you compliment a boxer?
Tell him he's a knock-out.

How do you compliment a witch?
Tell her she's charming.

How do you compliment
an astronaut?
Tell her she's out of this world.

Why do pencils make
good lawyers?

They always make their points.

*

What do you call a woman who
builds wire fences?

Barb.

*

What does a lizard like to
eat with his burger?

Curly flies.

Why did Jerry move his bed to
the woods after tossing and
turning at home?

So he could sleep like a log.

＊

Who slept in a traffic jam for
100 years?

Beeping Beauty.

＊

How do fish weigh themselves?

They stand on their scales.

＊

What does Tarzan say about
swinging through the jungle?

"It's de-vine!"

323

Why was the tree released from prison?

It decided to turn over a new leaf.

*

What doesn't have a body, but has two legs and runs?

A pair of pantyhose.

*

How do girl pigs wear their hair?

In people-tails.

*

How do horses wear their hair?

In ponytails.

What do a cat, an author, and a kite have in common?

They all have tails.

*

What do you call a royal seabird?

A regal segull.

What do a kangaroo, a dress, and
a parachutist have in common?

They're all jumpers.

*

What do a mother deer, a baker,
and a banker have in common?

They all have a little doe.

*

Did you hear about the girl who
bought perfume from a skunk?

*She fell for it…hook, line
and stinker.*

*

Why did the girl put bandages on
her bedroom window?

She was told the window had pains.

HOW DO YOU FIRE...?

How do you fire watch
repair people?

Tell them their time is up.

How do you fire teachers?

Tell them they're dismissed.

How do you fire authors?

Tell them it's The End.

How do you fire lumberjacks?

Give them the ax.

How does a cowboy cross
the ocean?

On his seahorse.

What do you call a girl who gets
up early?

Dawn.

*

When are most twins born?

On Twos-day.

*

What do you call the best student
at the octopus school?

A goody eight-shoes.

*

Why did Peg Leg the Pirate lose
control over his crew?

He couldn't put his foot down.

21.
I'm Out of Here!

How fast do happy bikers ride?
Ten smiles per hour.

What's the best thing to take
on a hot bike trip?
A thirst-aid kit.

Where do grizzlies put their bike bells?

On the handlebears.

*

What does a tornado do with a new car?

Takes it out for a spin.

*

What does a teacher do with a new car?

Gives it a test drive.

*

What vegetable can you use to polish your car?

Wax beans.

How does a kangaroo start
a dead battery?

With jumper cables.

*

What's the best fuel to put in
your lawn mower?

Grassoline.

*

Why don't mummies
take vacations?

*They're afraid they'll
relax and unwind.*

*

Why did it take so long for the
bride to walk down the aisle?

She had a train on her dress.

GET GOING!

What do you say to a slow walnut?

"Get cracking!"

What do you say to a
slow taxidermist?

"Do your stuff!"

What do you say to a slow
pencil sharpener?

"Get to the point!"

What do you say to a slow pencil?

"Get the lead out!"

What do you say to a slow
rubber band?

"Make it snappy!"

Why are beavers like trains?
All day long they chew, chew, chew.

*

How can you get your dog
to board a locomotive?
Train it.

*

In which part of a train
do ghosts ride?
The caBOOse.

CAR TUNES

What did the jack say to the car?

"Can I give you a lift?"

What did the driver say
to the rabbit?

"Hop in!"

What did one tire say to
the other tire?

"Want to go around together?"

What did the bumper say
to the fender?

"I had a smashing time today."

What did the wiper say to the
windshield?

"What's bugging you today?"

What did the car say to the bridge?

"You make me cross!"

How is a firefly like a car?

They both have taillights.

Who should you call if you don't
feel like paddling your own canoe?

A rowbot.

*

What do kings ride around
their castles?

Moatercycles.

*

What's a cow's favorite
amusement park ride?

The dairy-go-round.

*

What do gorillas love at
a playground?

The monkey bars.

Why do cows take nonstop flights?

They love the long moooovies.

Who would you call to perform
in a sea circus?

The clown fish.

When is it dangerous to be in the
ocean up to your ankles?

When you're upside down.

BYE-BYE!

How do you say good-bye
to a crocodile?

"Later, alligator!"

How do you say good-bye
to a yardstick?

"So long!"

How do you say good-bye
to a bad cold?

"Catch you later!"

How do you say good-bye
at the mall?

"Buy-buy!"

How do you say good-bye
to an ocean?

Don't say anything…just wave.

Index

A

Aardvarks, 78
Abominable Snowman. *See* Bigfoot and Abominable Snowman
Air, 14
Airplanes, 35, 67, 76, 244
Alligators and crocodiles, 36–38, 108, 121, 342
Angels, 62, 175, 178, 256
Animal books, 46
Animals. *See specific animals*
Ants, 20, 23
Apes, 279. *See also* Chimps; Gorillas; Monkeys
Astronauts, 74, 79, 98, 290, 294–295, 320
Authors, 325, 327

B

Babies, 146
Bakers, 117, 184, 233, 280, 326
Ballet, 86
Bambi, 211
Bananas, 265, 311
Band, 142–143, 195

Baseball, 57, 75, 76, 145, 152, 197, 284
Basketball, 59, 124, 147, 202
Bathtime laughs, 237–263
Bats, 317. *See also* Dracula; Vampires
Beach boys, 75
Beans, 115, 331
Bears, 112, 138, 156, 160, 211, 230, 241
Beavers, 83, 334
Bedtime jokes, 265–288
Bees, 6, 20, 22, 40, 54, 69, 148, 159, 169, 173, 185, 223, 245, 260, 308
Beetles, 18, 32
Beggar, 280
Belts, 76, 211, 270, 293
Bicycle, 26
Bigfoot and Abominable Snowman, 207–208, 242, 320
Bikes, 330–331
Billboards, 170
Billy the Kid, 232
Biologists, 63, 70
Birds, 125, 239, 271. *See also specific birds*
Birthdays, 52, 176–183, 187, 197
Blob, 213

Boats, 223, 228, 234, 244, 338

Body parts, 198–199, 225

Boomerang, 82

Boxing and boxers, 81, 273, 320

Bread, 7, 233, 280

Breakfast, 7, 8, 206–207, 213, 294

Brooms, 6, 175, 208, 219, 220

Bubble gum, 32, 69

Butterflies, 22, 23, 48, 90, 154

C

Cake, 76, 115, 177–179, 182, 206, 251

Camelot, 231

Camels, 152

Canaries, 8

Cards, 53, 149

Carpenters, 70, 76, 84, 179

Carrots, 121, 172, 177

Cars, 36, 61, 163, 211, 282, 331, 336–337

Caterpillars, 154

Cats, 8, 43, 46, 52, 90, 165, 197, 223, 316, 325. *See also* Leopards; Tigers

Celebration books, 187

Cell phone, 241

Centipedes, 62, 226, 249

Cheerleaders, 8, 55

Cheetahs, 51, 53

Chickens, 59

Chickens and roosters, 42, 51–52, 87, 96

Chimney sweeps, 168

Chimps, 28, 112. *See also* Apes; Gorillas; Monkeys

Cinderella, 147, 227, 228–229, 307

Clams, 22, 54

Cleopatra, 278

Clocks, 10–12, 20, 101

Clones, 128, 169, 223

Colds, 76, 127, 134, 155, 274, 342

Compliments, 320

Computer program(mers), 84, 256, 286

Computers, 77–87, 195, 221, 275, 286

Constellations, 293, 295

Contractor, 72

Cookbooks, 114

Corn, 99, 101, 116, 118, 206, 239

Couch potatoes, 50, 99

Cowboys, 110, 259, 288, 328

Cows, 47, 111, 131, 179, 181,

233, 236, 283, 291, 298, 301, 338, 339
Crabs, 5, 54, 191
Crayfish, 47
Crocodiles. *See* Alligators and crocodiles
Crows, 116, 161
Crusoe, Robinson, 228
Cyclops, 111

D

Dandruff, 130
Deer, 31, 59, 211, 326
Demons, 177, 204
Dentists, 13, 122, 123, 132, 234
Dinosaurs, 58, 203
Diploma, 261
Divers, 68, 70, 178
Doctors, 13, 124, 125, 131, 132, 134, 142, 149, 154, 198
Dogs, 9, 12, 44, 46, 235, 259, 275, 303, 314, 316, 334
Dolphins, 41–42
Dracula, 197, 210, 211, 213, 223. *See also* Vampires
Dragons, 92, 122
Dreams, 305, 307–310, 312
Dressing, 110–111, 207, 266
Drivers and driving, 8, 22, 67, 89, 282, 336

Ducks, 13, 44, 141, 165, 176, 226, 302. *See also* Rubber duckies
Dumbbell, 157
Dwarfs, 178

E

Eagles, 115
Eels, 33, 201
Eggs, 9, 42, 66, 101, 206, 287
Einstein, 71, 72, 260
Electrician, 72
Elephants, 35, 227, 239, 268, 280, 300
Elvis, 278
E-mail, 86–87, 196
Engines, 73, 77, 247
Extraterrestrials and aliens, 200, 213, 295. *See also* UFOs
Eyes, 17, 81, 94, 111, 199, 270

F

Fairies, 193, 226, 230, 234
Fairy tails, freaky, 227–236
Falcons, 156
Farmers, 64, 66, 78, 116, 173, 317
Fathers, 118, 144, 218, 244
Fireflies. *See* Lightning bug

and fireflies
Firing people, 327
Fish, 51, 80–81, 97, 105, 147, 149, 243, 278, 322, 340
Flamingos, 58
Fleas, 18, 126, 201
Flowers, 17, 24, 34, 69, 137, 281
Food, funny, 98–121. *See also specific foods*
Four-leaf clover, 302
Frankenstein, 222, 225
Frogs, 55, 57, 109, 155, 168, 197, 305, 315
Fruit, 40, 105, 113, 247, 265, 311

G

Games & groans, 147–157
Garbage, 57
Garbage cans, 46
Garbage man, 315
Genes, 63, 128, 169
Ghosts, ghouls, and goblins, 126, 159, 195, 204, 206, 210, 211, 214, 216, 217, 218, 221–222, 254, 334
Giraffes, 40, 241
Gloves, 69, 135, 173
Goats, 299, 312
Godfather, 244

Golfers, 94, 270
Good-bye, 342–343
Goose, 243
Gorillas, 212, 316, 338. *See also* Apes; Chimps; Monkeys
Grass, 290, 332
Grasshoppers, 153
Gulls, 176, 325

H

Hair, 89, 121, 130, 170, 184–185, 209, 215, 218, 252, 266, 292, 324
Hamburgers, 174
Hamlet, 176
Hands, 10, 69, 95, 135, 173, 254
Headless Horseman, 236
Heart, 149, 198
Hockey players, 277, 312
Homework, 23, 36, 90, 115
Horror books, 224–225
Horses, 96, 129, 184, 236, 324
Hot dogs, 102, 202
Hummingbirds, 36
Hurricanes, 59, 80

I

Ice cream, 112–113, 235
Insects, 18, 20, 316. *See also* specific insects

J

Japanese people, 273
Jeans, 66, 200, 204
Jellyfish, 34
Joggers, 252, 280
Judges, 61, 268

K

Kangaroos, 36, 50, 162, 181,
 272, 326, 332
Karate, 76
Kenobi, Obi-Wan, 7
Kent, Clark, 228
Kermit the Frog, 305
Ketchup, 70, 81
Kings, 205, 231, 269, 338
Kites, 115, 325
Knights, 231–232, 318

L

Lacrosse games, 153
Ladybugs, 18, 48
Lambs. See Sheep
Lamp, 63
Lawn mower, 332
Lawyers, 272, 321
Leopards, 80, 170, 239, 248
Library books, 65
Lifeguard, 74
Lightning bugs, 14

Lightning bugs and fireflies,
 201–202, 337
Lipstick, 69, 165
Liver, 198
Lizards, 38, 321
Lobsters, 19, 33
Lumberjacks, 22, 61, 327

M

Mall madness, 158–171
Man in the moon, 292–293
Marriage and weddings, 27,
 117, 172–176, 259, 332
Math, 33, 73, 89, 91, 96
Medical books, 128
Medicine cabinet, 133
Meteors, 292, 295
Mice, 8, 43–44, 46, 52, 150,
 177, 202, 238
Mickey Mouse, 61, 238
Milk, 52, 119, 121, 291
Ministers, 76, 257
Mistakes, 65, 85
Mona Lisa, 315
Monkeys, 298, 301. See also
 Apes; Chimps; Gorillas
Monsters, 190–191, 204,
 212. See also Frankenstein
Moon, 289–295
Moose, 31, 32
Mother Nature, 284

Moths, 48, 90
Mountains, 24, 26, 28, 82, 287
Mouth, 199
Movies, 47, 144, 197, 220, 284, 308, 309, 339
Mozart, 274, 319
Mummies, 127, 205, 217, 255, 310, 332
Music, 48, 89, 136–145, 195, 219, 274. *See also* Songs and singing
Mussels, 22, 34
Mystery writers, 317

N

Nature books, 22
Neptune, 34
Nuts, 7, 73, 148, 319, 333

O

Ocean. *See* Sea and ocean
Octopus, 95, 254, 329
Ogres, 192. *See also* Monsters
Old Mother Hubbard, 235
Old Woman Who Lived in a Slipper, 232
Omaha, Nebraska, 318
Opera stars, 257
Owl, 305

Oysters, 33, 181, 279
Oz, 228

P

Pajamas, 210, 268, 269, 272
Pantyhose, 324
Paper towel, 82
Parrots, 40
Parties, 54, 182, 187, 188
Pelicans, 176
Penguins, 99, 101
Pets, 16, 46. *See also specific animals*
Pheasants, 307
Photographers, 118
Pianos/pianists, 123, 144–145, 219
Piggy banks, 26, 93
Pigs and hogs, 28, 47, 57, 66, 71, 93, 163, 173, 185, 308, 312, 324
Pioneers, 276
Pirates, 210, 329
Pizza, 60, 109, 114
Planes. *See* Airplanes
Plates, 116
Plumbers, 257, 261
Police, 25, 70, 71, 119, 152, 179, 251, 262–263, 296
Popeye, 110
Porcupine, 106, 113

Post office workers, 309
Potatoes, 64, 78, 99, 106, 115, 207
Princess, 66
Prom night, 184–185

R

Rabbits, 30, 38, 126, 170–172, 177, 251, 258, 336
Radish, 266
Rhyming riddles, 316
Robes, 38, 210, 268
Robins, 182
Robots, 261
Rock stars/groups, 253, 308, 309
Rubber duckies, 228, 240, 242

S

Sailors, 62, 160, 240
Saints, 178
Salad, 99, 110–111
Salt, 69, 105
Sandwiches, 106, 246
Santa Claus, 59, 116, 152, 186, 222, 236
Scary creatures, 203–226
School, 6, 14, 41, 65, 88–97, 115, 137, 265, 329
Scientists, 63, 72, 201. See

also Biologists
Scorpions, 202
Scuba divers. See Divers
Sea and ocean, 32, 34, 49, 201, 284, 328, 341, 343
Sea creatures, 52. *See also specific sea animals*
Sea horses, 34, 328
Seals, 38
Sharks, 9, 13, 54, 56, 245
Sheep, 36, 47, 169, 296–299
Shoes and sneakers, 69, 160, 161, 164, 232, 266, 329
Shopping, 158–171
Shopping books, 164
Shower, 65, 228, 248, 250, 251, 252–257, 258–259, 260, 292, 297
Silly Billy, 29, 113, 242, 244, 246, 249–250, 265, 267, 27
Silly Sarah, 6, 30–31, 242, 266, 272, 277, 282, 305, 30
Silly Smoochies, 69
Sir Galahad, 231–232
Sir Lancelot, 92, 231
Sister, 65
Skeletons, 143, 182, 198, 213, 219
Skunks, 40, 58, 158, 161, 238, 315, 326
Skydiver, 62

Skywalker, Luke, 7
Sleeping bag, 288
Slippers, 227, 232, 242,
   265–266
Slow things, 333
Slugs, 193, 201, 283
Snacks, 114, 118, 201
Snails. *See* Slugs
Snakes, 27, 51, 125, 202,
   299, 301
Sneezes, 42, 76, 84, 131
Snowboarder, 74
Snowmen, 83, 320
Snow White, 61
Socks, 127, 270
Songs and singing, 129, 138,
   140, 144, 182, 254–257
Space/spaceship, 47, 79,
   291, 298
Spaghetti, 98, 102, 307
Spiders, 48, 86, 101, 154,
   175, 186, 196, 226, 236
Spy, 276
Squids, 302
Squirrels, 73, 176
Steel workers, 256
Streams, 97, 159
Submarine pilots, 74
Surfers, 151
Swamps, 36, 118
Swamp Thing, 216

T

Tails, 165, 301, 324, 325
Tarzan, 322
Teachers, 73, 132, 237, 331.
   See also School
Teeth, 29, 31, 32, 122–124,
   128, 234
Tennis, 13, 151
Throat, 123, 199, 305
Tigers, 40, 82, 272, 284
Tinkerbell, 230
Toast, 264
Tony the Tiger, 272
Tooth Fairies, 234
Tornadoes, 150, 331
Trains, 134, 147, 334
Trapeze artists, 256
Travel agents, 309
Trees, 7, 16–17, 31, 61, 113,
   140, 173, 324
Trolls, 192–193, 195
Turkeys, 58, 100, 103, 143,
   185, 186
TV, 43, 241, 283
Twins, 329

U

UFOs, 224. *See also*
   Extraterrestrials
Umpires, 76
Unicorns, 191

V

Vampires, 44, 205, 207, 210, 216, 223. *See also* Dracula
Vegetables, 106, 109, 114, 115, 120, 128, 206, 331
Veterinarians, 154

W

Wacky books
  animal books, 46
  celebration books, 187
  computer books, 85
  cookbooks, 114
  horror books, 224–225
  library books, 65
  nature books, 22
  shopping books, 164
Waiters, 106, 151, 309
Websites, 80–82
Werewolves, 188, 209, 217–218, 222, 225
Whales, 49, 300
Witches, 147, 175, 195–196, 206, 208, 214–216, 217, 219–220, 320
Wizard, 214
Workouts, 147–148
Worms, 6, 14, 15, 166, 232, 271

Y

Yard, 162, 342
Yogi, 276

Z

Zebras, 283
Zombies, 218
Zookeepers, 118
Zorro, 56, 274